TOM DADDARIO
AND ED ZOLLER

A LEADER'S HANDBOOK FOR SUCCESS

17 Traits of a Successful Leader

OTHER BOOKS
BY TOM DADDARIO

The Path to Success in New Home Sales

*The Next Step in Becoming a Top Producer
in New Home Sales (Coming Soon)*

Print ISBN: 978-1-66782-252-5
eBook ISBN: 978-1-66782-253-2

Printed in the United States of America

TABLE OF CONTENTS

ACKNOWLEDGEMENTS

(TD) I want to thank the Lord
for his gifts and blessings.

I want to thank my wife and son
for all their support and encouragement.

I want to thank my friend and co-author Ed Zoller
for his insight and input.

FORWARD

When I first came up with the idea to write a book on Leadership, I asked my friend Ed Zoller if he would proofread the book for me. His insights and suggestions were so impressive that I suggested we form a partnership and write this book together.

Throughout the book you will see notations for me (TD) and for Ed (EZ) that indicate the sections we each authored.

A little background on me (TD):

My leadership experience for this book stems from the new home industry. I have been in this environment since 1989 and in leadership since 1998. After being a department leader for several decades I decided to take a step back and return to the sales floor in December of 2017. It has been interesting, to say the least, to observe the leaders of the company and perhaps that observation is what motivated me to finish this book. I work for a wonderful, Christian led home builder in a top selling community. From a construction standpoint we are hands down, the best builder in the area as evidenced by our over 100 4 – 5-star Google reviews. However, in the 4 years I have been here we have **never** hit our sales goals. The sales team has always been the blame for the shortfall which of course is not the reason. I suspect we are not the only company in this situation and hopefully this book will help real leaders rethink the way they run their business.

A little background on ED:

Ed started his career while he was a full-time student, working part time at a small Midwest chain of lumberyards, where he quickly moved from warehouseman to sales to management. He then went to work for a mid-size distributor of residential, commercial, and industrial plumbing products. At that distributor, he managed sales teams, helped design showrooms, and created sales programs for plumbers and their builders.

Following that, he worked for the second-largest buying cooperative in the US, where he started in regional sales, was promoted to sales management, and then moved to creating sales and marketing programs. His was promoted to Vice President of Purchasing, where he managed a team of 50 purchasing professionals, covering over $1.4 billion in annual spend.

His next move was to one of the largest builders in the US, where he was Vice President of Strategic Sourcing. His corporate team structured purchasing agreements covering $3 billion in annual spend. He then transitioned to a regional purchasing role for another large residential builder. As a pre-retirement activity, Ed took on a sales role, where he won numerous awards as a site agent selling new homes.

One common thread throughout Ed's career has been designing and executing training programs for sales, purchasing, negotiating, and public speaking. He has a BA in Pre-Law and an MBA.

INTRODUCTION

Having worked for the best leaders and the worst bosses (and everything in between) I (TD) decided to share some observations and techniques that have resulted in success, both as a manager and a leader. I read many books on management and leadership and always try to utilize the best ideas. After years of trial and error and success with a variety of management and leadership techniques, this book distills many of my experiences.

For the experienced managers and leaders, we hope this handbook acts as a refresher course. Even better, perhaps it will spark a few new ideas. From my (EZ) perspective, the best outcome of your reading this book is that you will find enough value to pass it on to your teams.

To those new to management and leadership, I hope this book will help you avoid the pitfalls I (TD) have experienced first-hand and those I have heard about while comparing notes with other managers and leaders. I also hope you will pick up some tips on how you can grow from being a "boss" to effectively managing, and even leading, your team to success.

When Ed and I started this book, the year was 2012 and we were just coming out of what is now called the "Great

Recession". To say life in the US has changed would be an immense understatement. We are still in the throes of the Covid 19 Pandemic and the challenges leaders are now faced with are opposite than the challenges of the Great Recession. One example is the employment situation. During the Great Recession leaders struggled with how to keep talented employees versus today the challenge is finding talented employees. According to the US Bureau of Labor Statistics in August of 2021 there were 10.4 million job openings compared to 6.4 million only one year ago.

If there ever was a need for strong, flexible corporate leadership, it is now. In today's workforce not only is a manager faced with the normal challenges of hiring high producers, providing training, motivating, mentoring and retaining top talent, today's leader is faced with a number of new challenges.

One of those new challenges is and will continue to be 'doing more with less'.

Most companies have learned to do a lot more with a lot less and consequently many workers are doing double or even triple duty. This was true during the Great Recession and, for different reasons, is true during the Covid 19 Pandemic.

As the economy changes, the challenges also change and evolve. As a Manager and Leader, you need to change with the times and the circumstances if you intend to stay employed and be of service to your team and a profit generator for your employer.

A commonly held theory is that companies evolve as follows: from survival to stability, stability to success and success to significance. (Zig Ziglar, *Over the Top - From*

Survival to Significance). My observation is that today most businesses are somewhere between survival and stability; unfortunately, many have accepted this condition as the new normal. Occasionally, you see a company that is between stability and success or has even arrived at success. Have you ever wondered what the determining factors were that separates the companies that are barely making it and the ones that are enjoying success? The answer is quite simple; it all goes back to leadership.

To clarify some terms, we use in this book, this is what we mean when we use the word:

Boss or Supervisor: the person you must report to in the chain of command.

Manager: in the classic Business School definition, the person who is responsible for the short- and long-term business functions of Plan-Organize-Develop-Control

Leader: the person who goes a step beyond the managerial functions of Plan-Organize-Develop-Control by having the unique ability to engender trust and respect from his/her team. The Leader will typically earn that same trust and respect from peers and upper management. The Leader's team will likely be more results-driven and performance-focused than most Managers or Bosses.

If you have spent much time in the ranks of the employed, I am sure you have witnessed Managers who were proficient technocrats but who were unable to inspire the team to peak performance. You have probably also worked for Supervisors who had weak people skills yet always got the reports in on time. You may have also experienced Leaders who could inspire you to scale any height but had an aversion to the details of implementation.

In reality, if you are in a position of responsibility for staff, you probably exhibit the traits of Boss/Manager/Leader in varying degrees and at various times. We all tend to migrate from role to role based on circumstance, skill set, temperament, and training. As we move from zone to zone, we exhibit different traits.

Management and Leadership skills are such a mixed bag that I hesitate to use the word "charisma" because it can confuse the student of Leadership. While a winning personality is very important to managing and leading, not every Leader has that magic "charisma". Nor can we all aspire to learn it or earn it.

If you have been employed for any significant length of time, you have experienced supervisors who have many excellent skills, but who may also have serious deficiencies. For example, you may have worked for someone who functions well one-on-one or in small meetings, but who appears to be incompetent in front of large groups. You may have worked with someone who thinks in terms of words, tables, and graphs, but cannot construct a spreadsheet to save his soul. Despite these deficiencies, these supervisors may have been terrific managers or even great leaders because they have mastered the movement from the zones of supervision to management to leadership.

Obviously, the most productive and successful employees and business owners will learn to spend more time in the 'zone of leadership', while paying due attention to the needs of supervision and management.

This Handbook will give you some refreshers on the traits of the Top Leaders so you can grow to be more successful in your role as a Leader.

CHAPTER 1

The Best (and worst) Leadership Traits

Look at the list of questions below and note which behavioral traits best describes you.

1. Do you lead by example or are you duplicitous?

2. Are you truthful or do you resort to "truthiness"?

3. Are you transparent or mysterious?

4. Is your agenda open and understandable or obscure?

5. Are you afraid to hire people smarter than you?

6. Do you leverage your employees' strengths, or do you handcuff them?

7. Do you catch them doing things right or doing things wrong?

8. Do you give credit or grab credit?

9. Do you praise in public and punish in private?

10. Do you encourage or undercut your direct reports?

11. Are you a cheer leader or a buzz killer?

12. Do you elevate people up or hold them down?

13. Is a 90% effort acceptable or are you the only one who can contribute 100%?

14. Are you able to get tasks accomplished simply by asking or do you resort to manipulation and/or coercion?

15. Do you encourage open dialog or is it "my way or highway"?

16. Do you promote a team environment, or do you encourage conflict among your team?

17. Are you grateful for the results you get from your team, or do you believe it is expected?

If you selected a member of your team who you especially respect, how would they describe you in light of these traits?

You and your direct reports need to take the survey (Appendix 1) at the back of the book. For the best results, have them take it anonymously and hand it in to your administrative assistant; that person can put together the results in one report for you to review.

Hopefully, you lead according to the positive trait descriptions on the left side of the above list, but you need to be sure. Did the survey reveal any discrepancies, how will you respond: with anger or an open mind? Are you willing to take the journey to becoming a Leader? Are you willing to make the effort to operate in the "Zone of Leadership"?

At my (TD) first job in the home building industry, I worked for the *worst* boss I ever had. He had all the managers read a book on leadership and at the time I was in my 20' and pretty naïve; the author actually believed a good leader should behave according to the negative behaviors on right side of the list. This author seemed to be a proponent of the school of management that contends it is better to be feared than respected. I sincerely believed my boss directed us read this book to demonstrate what we should NOT do as his managers.

Unfortunately, I was wrong! I quickly learned that I was working for a very confused human being. Apparently, he had a very challenging upbringing that contributed to his negative management style. His dysfunctional behaviors were fraught with negative traits. The main thing I learned from his management style was what NOT to do.

Conversely, I worked for an amazing leader who truly believed in the positive behaviors on the left where I observed firsthand the positive results. Due to her leadership, we typically met or exceeded our goals in a very challenging corporate environment. In fact, those who were part of that team still refer to it as the dream team many years later.

Some of the traits in the list might seem idealistic to you as they once did to me. However, if you learn to foster these positive behaviors in yourself and in your team, you will almost certainly build a team that will rise above the competition. And more importantly you will enjoy life a whole lot more. I imagine the prospect of less worrying, less heartburn, better sleep and maximizing your success, profits and income is something you find attractive. If my guess is right, read on.

Did you ever stop to consider what manager's top priorities are? Here are the four most important based on my experience and observation:

First and foremost, you are responsible for maximizing the company's profits and the value of its stock.

Second, you set the example, for implementing the corporate vision and culture for your team to follow. You are personally responsible to be certain the corporate culture and vision are communicated to your team in a manner that aligns with corporate goals and objectives.

Third, you must be able to remove the obstacles that lie in the path of success of those that report to you.

Fourth, be prepared to take responsibility for the team's shortcomings while giving them credit for their successes.

Those managers who focus on these priorities are typically operating more in the Zone of Leadership and have grown beyond the zones of Management and Supervision.

The roots of this leadership style are planted in the characteristics of integrity, honesty, humility, discipline, and sacrifice. I have observed that there is a diminishing effect from the top of the corporate ladder to the bottom. When the head of the company sets the bar extremely high, the amount of reduction at the lower rungs is minimal. However, if the corporate head lacks these characteristics, by the time you get to the lower rungs, there is not much moral substance to the team or the company. This holds true for the leader's enthusiasm, passion, and belief in the companies' products and services. Another way to think of this is imagine a bonfire. The bigger and hotter the flame the farther away you can get and still be warm, but a small flame only reaches the people that are standing next to it.

So, let's look at the 17 behavioral traits and why they are so important to understand if you want to hone your leadership skills.

CHAPTER 2

First Step - Look in the Mirror

These traits deal with basic character traits and how they influence your decisions. If you can't be honest with yourself about your shortcomings and your strengths, this book will likely be a bad investment. Self-evaluation is the vital foundation for improvement. If you can't deal with critical analysis from yourself, your employees, your co-workers, and your supervisor, you will find your career will be punishing.

1. Do you lead by example or are you duplicitous?

I (TD) have observed that the best leaders lead by example ALL the time and that they expect their team to follow in their footsteps. This includes everything from the exciting to the mundane. It is critical to remember all eyes are on you. You don't have the luxury of lowering your standards, no matter what the situation.

We have all had those occasions where emotions are running high or there seems to be some pressure for a snap decision or action. Those are the times we might say or do something we will regret. I heard a great saying once, "The greatest decisions that I regret were the ones I made when I was upset." To paraphrase something, I once read concerning the Alcoholics Anonymous program, 'Never make an important decision if you are hungry, angry, lonely, tired, or sick/scared (remember the acronym HALT[S])'. The point here is that very few decisions must be made on the spot; most can be made once all the parties have calmed down and you can take a step back from the situation to better analyze the facts.

This is another situation where your team (including your manager) will judge you based on your consistency and even-handed leadership style.

2. Are you truthful or do you resort to "truthiness"?

Are you honest to a fault, or do you believe that occasionally it is ok to lie? Do you believe that "situational ethics" can warrant the stretching of the truth?

How do you define a lie? When I was a kid, I was told a "white lie" was sometimes permissible. A white lie is a little lie. The problem with this is who determines the size of lie? Well, here is the truth: a lie is a lie and you either are honest or you are not. You cannot be honest part of time because by default that means you are dishonest part of the time.

Stephen Colbert coined the word "truthiness" to describe a situation that probably is not true, but somehow has the ring of truth. No matter how you slice it, truthiness is a distortion of truth. It is simply another form of lying.

How about this old saw: in business you must lie sometimes to be successful? This is another false belief. I have learned that you never have to lie. If you do lie or resort to truthiness, when you get caught you will destroy the trust of the person you lied . . . so just be truthful. There is immutable value to the old adage "honesty is the best policy."

In John Maxwell's book, *The 21 Irrefutable Laws of Leadership* he states, "Trust is the foundation of leadership." I (TD) have found this to be true both as a manager and a direct report. One thing I can attest to regarding trust is you can't fake it. If you are not trustworthy you will eventually be exposed.

As a final note on lying, there are two categories you need to be conscious of: compulsive and pathological lying. Both are symptomatic of deeper psychological issues that you are probably not trained to deal with. If your boss falls into one of these categories, your best course of action is to find another supervisor or find another job. You will never be comfortable or successful in this kind of environment.

If you have an employee who falls into this category, consult with your Human Resources Department and deal with the problem immediately. Your team likely knows when a co-worker is dishonest, and they will evaluate you based on how you deal with this dishonesty. Your tolerance of a bad co-worker will be interpreted as tacit permission of bad performance and will spread like a contagion if you do not deal with it fairly, quickly, and decisively.

Early in my (EZ) career, I was faced with a problem employee on a two-member team. "Sue" and "Karen" were closer than twin sisters and worked well together for years (or so it seemed). They were an incredibly productive duo. However, I became aware of a performance issue that came to light during an informal audit. It took me some time to determine which of the "sisters" was the cause of the problem. The issue was serious enough that it required an immediate dismissal for cause and "Karen" was literally escorted to the door.

I anticipated tears and the gnashing of teeth from "Sue". I sat down immediately after the dismissal and explained to "Sue" that certain issues had come to light and would not be tolerated. As a result, her "sister" had been terminated. To my amazement, "Sue" thanked me profusely for terminating "Karen". "Sue" said that while she loved "Karen" dearly, she did not feel comfortable to reveal Karen's dishonesty. "Sue" was greatly relieved and her already solid performance actually improved.

3. Are you transparent or mysterious?

By transparent, I am referring to how open you are to your direct reports about your concerns, feelings, and goals?

I (EZ) once worked for a person who was so erratic and unpredictable that I never knew what he really expected of me. He would give me a glowing performance review and then communicate to his supervisor that I was not running my team properly. He would give me a verbal order to do one thing, and then immediately send me an email with instructions that were totally in opposition to his verbal direction. Fortunately, I had a better relationship with HR than he did, so I was able to protect myself. His mysterious behavior ultimately led to his removal, but not before many projects were in turmoil.

In another instance, I worked closely with the head of HR on several assignments. It was common knowledge that when she wore black, someone was going to be fired. On the black days, everyone knew to avoid her, even if it was urgent. She was totally transparent, but not in a good way! Ironically, when she was not dressed in black, she was a good manager.

If you are open and clear with your team, they will feel comfortable in your relationship and will perform better as a result.

On the other hand, you must be wary of being too candid and overly friendly with your direct reports.

We believe you must set a boundary with your team because you can get too close and that may create problematic issues

Think of it this way: outside of work, you have your friends and family; at work, you have your business friends and colleagues. The best leaders seem to keep their personal life and their business life separate. More importantly, they are not afraid to share expectations and concerns with their team. In fact, this transparency often creates a very open, positive, productive discussion, even if there is bad news to share. There is nothing more counterproductive than having to worry if your boss has a secret agenda. This will shut down all hopes of having an open, honest, robust conversation. In his book, *Winning*, Jack Welch puts it this way, "Leaders establish trust with candor, **transparency** (emphasis mine), and credit."

4. Is your agenda open and understandable or obscure?

Honesty, consistency, and transparency are vital traits for a manager who aspires to true leadership. Having open agendas ties into the above traits in two different ways: first, you must have an open, understandable agenda, and second, you must be able to communicate this agenda.

Leaders lay out the company's goals, and then translates those goals into the objectives for his/her team. The leader encourages open feedback from their team. They get everyone onboard because everyone has the opportunity to have input on goal setting. I (TD) learned a long time ago that if a supervisor sets the employee's goals for them, those goals belong to the supervisor, not the employee. If you set the guidelines for the goals and let the individual set their goal, then they own it and are more likely to hit or exceed it.

It is important that the leader shares their personal goals as well. Once a team gels it's amazing how much extra effort, they will give to not only hit their goals but push to make sure their boss achieves his/her goals.

Conversely, if a team thinks the boss has a hidden agenda, they will never truly give 100% to achieve their personal goal, let alone the goal of their manager. Lacking a complete understanding due to an obscure agenda, the employee will not push hard for fear of being at cross-purpose with the team goal and/or the manager's goal.

As a corollary to the need for an understandable agenda, you must also be able to communicate that agenda clearly to the team. What makes perfect sense on paper needs to come alive to the employee in order to be executed per the plan.

I (EZ) worked for a corporation that did an excellent job on short- and long-range planning. The articulated plan covered strategy, tactics, and logistics for nearly $3 billion in annual volume. The plan was broken down into every division, every department, every manager, and every employee. However, the Executive Staff did not consider the planning finished and executed until the managers and employees could articulate the plan on an individualized basis. It was often the starting discussion point of departmental meetings. It was not unusual for the C-level team to stop an employee in the hall or in the field and challenge the employee on their understanding of the plan and what their role was in the execution of that plan.

Even better, it was not unusual for the employee to return the challenge by asking the Executive staff member to clarify a point or to make a recommendation for the betterment of the plan!

Incidentally, I have worked for several companies who were able to articulate their strategic plan on the back of a business card. Another company used a two-sided laminated card that fit in the wallet just like a credit card. These statements of goals/strategic plan were short and sweet, and meant to be shared among employees, customers, and even vendors. Everyone had a laser-like focus on the goals of the company and understood how they fit into the achievement of those goals.

If you need help to sharpen your communication skills, don't hesitate to ask your manager or HR department for some direction and resources. If your team does not understand the company goals, your agenda, your goals, and especially their personal goals, your effectiveness will be significantly hampered.

5. Are you afraid to hire people smarter than you?

Of all the traits, this one truly separates the outstanding from the average. It takes a very grounded personality to admit you don't know everything or that your ideas may be good but not the best. Many bosses I (TD) have worked for have had huge egos, yet they lived in constant worry and fear of being "found out" by those above their rank as well as below. They were fearful of being eclipsed by their employees. They rarely hired people smarter than themselves and consequently never maximized their own potential, not to mention the potential of the company or the employee.

On a separate note, I (TD) read this post on a social media feed, and it really underscores the harm with a huge ego: "I have learned that it's better to drop the ego than to break a relationship. My ego will keep me aloof, whereas with relationships, I will never be alone." (Author unknown.)

You must hire staff that will challenge you, complement your weaknesses, and quite often, be much smarter than you are!

Early in my (TD) career I worked for a brilliant man who made his fortune taking over failed businesses. He targeted these businesses because, in his analysis, they failed chiefly because of poor leadership. He shared this observation with me: weak managers hire weak workers because it's the only way they can control them. He told me that in almost 100% of the businesses he took over, he eventually replaced the entire management staff. Think about all the businesses that are failing not because of their products services or business plan, but rather because of their lack of proper management!

Conversely the "Dream Team" I (TD) referred to earlier was made up of a group of the most talented managers I have ever worked with. If any department had a challenge they could not figure, out we would all come together and almost always come up with a solution. This kind of team works best when the leader is not afraid to hire the best, and then encourages them to be open and challenging with themselves and the rest of the team.

As leaders we tend to hire people with similar beliefs and values, however, we need to careful not to hire clones of ourselves. I was told once that if one of your managers agrees with you on everything then you don't really need that person. While weak managers may see a lack of agreement as a sign of disloyalty or discord, it is by far the preferred relationship if you ever hope to maximize the company's potential.

In fact, I (EZ) think the situation that yields the best results is to have team members that range from pessimistic to optimistic, from critic to cheerleader, and with various levels of experience. Both the Rookie and the Pro should be encouraged to air fresh opinions and ideas. This way all the potential risks and rewards would be presented and openly discussed so that the leader could make the best decision for the company. This discussion will also help the team evaluate options and see your management style in action. This process need not be democratic, but it does need to reflect that those diverse perspectives will be considered as you reach a decision. As you review your decision with the team, you will gain buy-in as you show them how their input shaped your decision.

Finally, when you have assembled your own "dream team", let them know you have high expectations of them and that you are confident in their ability to perform at a very high level.

In an interview, Peter Drucker said, "The toughest decisions are people decisions: hiring, firing, and promoting people. They receive the least attention and are the hardest to **unmake**. Seventy to ninety percent of a manager's success is based on these decisions"

Another key to being a successful leader is to hire the right person for the position as well as for the company. In his book, *Good to Great*, Jim Collins indicated that great leaders, "first got the right people on the bus, the wrong people off the bus, and the right people in the right seats – and then figure out where to drive it." He further states, "The old adage "People are your most important asset" turns out to be wrong. People are not your most important asset. The right people are."

Given the challenge and cost of hiring the best, many companies are trying to control overhead by using existing staff in lieu of new hires. The current staff may be less expensive than adding staff, yet the current staff may not have the bandwidth to cover more responsibilities. In the spirit of doing more with less, we "hope" the existing employee can "stretch" to fit the needs of additional assignments. However, without the appropriate skill set, training, and support, this "hope" is likely to turn into an expensive disappointment.

During the Great Recession an odd decision was made by most of the large builders in the US, in an attempt to economize on staffing they rolled up divisional tasks into the regional level in the hope of managing by long-distance. The result of this roll-up was that Divisional offices closed, and staff was discharged. The economies are often false due to on-going lease commitments, employee separation agreements, long-distance commuting by replacement staff, etc. However, in the short and intermediate term, expenses might appear to be cut. In the long term, these savings are often an illusion. Once the recession was over companies had to restaff, re-lease office space, and rebuild the Division at a high cost. In the end many very talented hires were lost to other opportunities.

While qualifications are important in today's work environments, fit, is equally important. So how do you go about hiring the right person? There is no 100% sure fire way but there are ways to mitigate the risks. I (TD) have found that if you have several people interview the candidate, have very specific questions to ask, have them take a personality assessment and most importantly do a thorough background check you raise the odds to about 85%. Regarding the background check, always speak to the candidate's prior bosses; never just check the references they give you. Also, much can be learned from a candidate's social media pages. I am often amazed at the things people post on their pages then can't understand why they never get hired.

One final note, in almost all the leadership books I have read there is one constant, the most important character trait to seek when hiring is integrity in the candidate. As those books will also tell you, 'Hire for attitude and train for aptitude'.

How to hire the best (EZ)

Here are some recommendations on how to improve the odds in your hiring decisions:

1. Have several others interview your finalist candidates. They should be people whose opinions you respect and who represent positions above, equal, and below the candidate. I often used managers from different departments to give me a perspective on candidates. When I was in Sales and Marketing, I occasionally called on a friend in Finance who was exceptionally good at reading candidates. A break for coffee or lunch is often a good time to have an informal interview with a manager from a different department and in a different environment.

2. Compile a list of favorite interview questions and use them consistently. I have a list of questions that are Industry and position specific. I allot a set time for every interview and try to ask the same questions in the same order every time. This frees me to record the candidates' responses for later analysis and comparison. I usually listen to the candidate answer to the question as well as how they process the question. Observing the eyes and body language during the interview is just as important as listening to the voice and the answers.

3. Coordinate testing with your HR Department. Personality assessments and position-specific skills testing can be very informative about candidates, although you must follow the HR guidelines

for consistency and to avoid potential liability. Keep in mind that you are hiring for attitude and can later determine the candidate's potential to be trained for aptitude.

4. Coordinate background checks with your HR Department. Credit checks, arrest and court records, and interviews with current and prior employers can be very informative. If possible, personally conduct these interviews. This is another area where your HR Department can give you assistance, especially since these checks and interviews may have liability potential. Incidentally, candidate references from friends, relatives, clergy, teachers, neighbors, etc. are rarely worth your time.

I (EZ) once worked at a very successful company with an incredible CEO; he was probably the best Leader I have personally experienced. In a very self-effacing manner, he would explain that he considered himself to be a "C" student who was very good at putting "A" students on his team to counterbalance his shortcomings.

How do you know if your candidate is truly smarter than you are? You need to create standards and job descriptions that are detailed and exhaustive. You need to execute employee testing, metrics, and interviews that are demanding, professional, consistent, and thorough. If the open position is highly placed with much responsibility, consider the use of third-party testing and interviewing. You will recoup the additional cost of hiring a third party by avoiding expensive hiring mistakes.

At every level of employment in this company, the CEO insisted on a rigorous testing and interviewing protocol, regardless of the position. If you were already an employee and were eligible for promotion, you were not exempt from the testing and interviewing. In fact, the higher the position, the more extensive the interview process. When I was eligible for an officer-level position, I was grilled for over three hours by an outside Industrial Psychologist whose favorite phrase was "hire smart or manage tough".

As a result, this CEO used various metrics and interviews to confirm that he was hiring people who were smarter than he was. In retrospect, that reveals him to be pretty darn smart!

The downside of finding and hiring top employees

As my (EZ) career evolved, I occasionally became frustrated over losing members of my team. "My" employees often left for other opportunities within the company (and occasionally outside the company). It became obvious that I was becoming a "feeder" to other divisions and departments as well as for promotions within my area.

As I shared my frustration with my HR liaison, she pointed out that my hiring and training process was bearing fruit for my team as well as the rest of the company. Other managers were learning to "cherry pick" my team for strong talent. The downside was my own heavy investment in finding, hiring, and training replacements. In light of the disruptions and costs to my team's effectiveness, I was successful in getting my boss to grant me a two-year moratorium against others stealing from my team. Needless to say, when there was significant need, this moratorium was happily suspended!

A similar situation happened to me (TD) during the Great Recession. My Division President moved to another builder and was forced to promote an internal candidate to the position of VP of Sales. Unfortunately, this person had no experience running a sales team and proceeded to "steal" my top sales agents with offers of better compensation. This VP was often heard bragging that he had the best sales team in the area. I took it as a backhand compliment. It all worked out as I ended up going to that company as the VP of Sales and got my team back!

Another downside to having a strong reputation for spotting and training talent is that you will be asked to evaluate employees who, for a variety of reasons, need to 'find another seat on the bus'. This can be a mixed blessing. More often than not, the employee in this situation was a questionable hire or put in the hands of a marginally capable supervisor. In these cases, another seat on the bus may help or may merely be a transition off the bus.

If you have the fortunate ability to re-train and re-direct the employee into the right seat on the bus, congratulate yourself on helping a deserving employee and saving the cost of finding and training a replacement employee.

Having a reputation for finding, training, and "saving" employees earned me (EZ) some degree of credibility. One of the upside benefits was the expansion of my personal network within the company and across divisions and departments.

CHAPTER 3

Getting the Most Out of Your Team

You are only as good as the people that report to you. The ego-centric manager mistakenly thinks he is the hero, when in reality, the Leader knows his success is attributable to his team.

The next seven categories deal with leveraging your team's strengths: by getting the most out each one and having fun along the way.

> 6. Do you leverage your employees' strengths, or do you handcuff them for fear it may make you look bad?

This goes hand in hand with having the self-confidence to hire employees that are smarter than you. Unfortunately, some managers stifle their team's potential for fear it may make them look weak. Their desire for self-preservation perversely blocks their ability to shine the light on an employee who could in turn make the manager look great. Ironically, helping the employee and the team shine would get the manager the credit for the team's success. This is the exact opposite outcome of what the weak manager fears. Instead of being eclipsed by his team, the team makes the manager look like a hero.

Some managers have never been taught how to develop and take advantage of their employees' strengths. Leveraging your strengths and your team's strengths is one of the easiest ways to be successful.

The weak manager handcuffs his team in many ways. He does not share resources or allocate information. He does not find educational and training opportunities for his team (or himself) that would aid growth. He interrupts employee presentations or injects himself into discussions in a way that discounts the contribution of his team.

7. Do you catch them doing things right or doing things wrong?

I (EZ) have worked for supervisors who were technically proficient at their jobs, but who lacked teaching skills. The best way to learn from them was to quietly observe and hope that there were no errors. When there were errors, they became magnified into "gotchas" that could take an hour to fix. The gotcha did not require that long to fix, except in the mind of the supervisor who lived for the opportunity to find a mistake and then review the error until my ears would bleed. The entire training regimen was reactive, and a good gotcha might be replayed several times over the next week, just to be certain the lesson would sink in.

Mature, functional people know when they make a mistake. Provided the corporate culture encourages a degree of risk taking, the person who made the mistake will usually bring the issue to the leader's attention along with several solutions. In this type of environment, it is not necessary for the manager to be aggressively on the hunt for mistakes since they are self-reported and often self-repaired.

However, if an employee has observed a supervisor that is standing by with an axe ready to chop off someone's head, they will never take risks and try to hide or pass blame for their mistakes. When you create an environment that acknowledges success and you let them know you are pleased with their performance, they will aspire to be more courageous and successful. This works well with raising kids too. I have heard people say they don't care about getting positive feedback, but I doubt this to be true; at some level we all yearn for recognition. In an article in Forbes titled, "What Employees Want More Than a Raise in 2012", the author quotes the following: "According to the Corporate Executive Board's quarterly study of 20,000 employees, money does not even rank in the top ten reasons that employees choose to remain in their jobs. The top five reasons for employee retention include: job-interest alignment, manager quality, co-worker quality, people management, and respect."

After you catch someone doing something right, take Tom Peter's advice and 'celebrate what you want to see more of' (*In* Search of Excellence).

8. Do you give credit or grab credit?

The higher the manager's self-confidence and self-esteem, the less inclined he will be to grab all the credit. To prove a point, I (TD) have even gone so far as to give all the credit to someone who took my idea and embellished it.

I was talking to a former employee recently and he shared that his current boss was a credit monger and then added, "I now realize how nice it was working with you because you always gave me all the credit and never took it for yourself." If you create the kind of team environment that engenders compelling, new ideas that improve the bottom line, your boss will know who to thank.

One negative effect of grabbing credit is that eventually the ideas just cease to develop; the company will stagnate and never reach its highest potential.

Another negative byproduct of credit mongering is the transference of blame to anyone but the leader. The inability to accept blame is analogous to the inability to accept responsibility. There is a well-known quote from Stephen W. Comisky that states, "You can delegate authority, but you can't delegate responsibility." A leader is ultimately responsible for everything that happens in their department.

Andrew Carnegie once said, "No man will make a great leader who wants to do it all himself or get all the credit for doing it." (This was originally stated in a 1902 biography about Carnegie, and it has been a bit revised since then.)

9. Do you praise in public and punish in private or the opposite?

If you want to shut down someone's performance quickly, chastise them in front of their peers. If you want to see someone bloom like a flower and reach for the sun, praise them in front of their peers. As simple as this is there are some supervisors that just don't get it. What they miss is that it's not just about chastising someone; it's often much more subtle.

Punishing in public can take many forms: Cutting someone off in a meeting, flashing a stern look, joking when someone offers a new idea, or rolling your eyes when they begin to speak. For some speakers, even an abrupt change of your body position can signal your displeasure or lack of interest. Always be aware of your body language when you are listening to an employee.

The secret to making this technique of public praise effective is to use it with discretion. If you openly praise too frequently, it loses its impact. Praise too little or too much and it comes across as insincere. Also, not all employees have the same "praise receptors" so you may have to customize it to each individual. When in doubt err on the conservative side, but then follow-up with a private word or note to reinforce the value of the employee's contribution. If you praise someone's performance, consider a note to the employee and a copy to the manager, with a comment on what was noteworthy.

When you do have a need to have a serious private discussion with an employee, consider the venue for that discussion very carefully. You should avoid using your office or the employee's office. Find a conference room that offers a few minutes of privacy. By avoiding the offices that are used daily, you will not have a negative feeling linger in a space that should be productive and positive, not a reminder of a corrective encounter. You will also avoid the gossip that 'Bob just got taken to the woodshed' or 'Andrea had to visit the principal's office'.

10. Do you encourage or undercut your direct reports?

Once an employee feels they have the trust of the boss their self-esteem and self-confidence soars. A manager who understands that mistakes are part of the learning process can encourage an employee to comfortably stretch past their normal comfort level. As an employee starts to stretch and take prudent risks, they come up with ideas that can positively impact the company's effectiveness and profitability. The litmus test on this one is simple, if seeing your employees reach their potential gives you a deep feeling of gratification, then you are on the right track. Create a safe environment for them to try new techniques, help them to take raw ideas and turn them into polished procedures or products. If they make a mistake along the way, don't crucify them, but rather work with them to identify what went wrong and assist them in coming up with alternatives. In his book *See you at the Top*, Zig Ziglar puts it this way, "The way you see your team members is the way you treat them and the way you treat them is the way they often become." In other words, do you see them as the best of the best or just mediocre? I will bet the ones you see as superstars are performing like superstars and unfortunately the same is true for the ones you see as mediocre. In *Winning*, Jack Welch believes the team will take cues from the leader regarding risk, "Leaders inspire risk taking and learning by setting the example."?

11. Are you a cheer leader or a buzz killer?

An effective leader needs to be the team's biggest cheer leader. The better you are at this the more it will pass on from your managers to their teams.

I (TD) was working for a company once and we were having a tough month in sales. The team rallied in the last week of the month with a strong finish but missed the sales goal. I sent an email to the sales team and copied my boss and the other supporting employees congratulating them on the Olympic effort they demonstrated that last week. Almost immediately my boss replied to everyone that the results for the month, "really sucked". What message do you think this sent to the entire team? Not only did it crush the sales team's spirits I never again copied my boss on that kind of message again. It was sad that one misguided supervisor could suck the life out of the team with one email. Bottom line, be a cheer leader, not buzz killer!

12. Do you push people up or hold them down?

One of the best bosses I ever had was a master at pushing the management team to incredible levels. I remember I had worked tirelessly on a project and had it just perfect. I proudly presented it to this boss and waited for the accolades. After reviewing my work this boss said, "This is really great, but you know what would make it even better?" I was a little put off because I had worked very hard and in my mind it was perfect. After I recovered from the lack of a standing ovation, I went to work on the suggested revision and ended up with an even better product, so good that I continue to use it today.

This is a great example of pushing employees up and challenging them in a positive, supportive manner.

Unfortunately, it doesn't always work this way. I had another boss who asked me to research why a particular community was not selling very well. After investing many hours of hard work, I submitted my report. The boss's response was, "This is completely wrong. Here is what I have concluded you need to do." There was no exchange of ideas, no analysis of my research, just a dictation of what he thought should happen next. Sadly, his conclusion was completely wrong, and the community never did regain sales momentum or profitability.

It never ceases to amaze me how much more you can get from an employee by simply treating them with respect and dignity. The Platinum Rule really holds true, "Treat others the way they want to be treated". The other problem with treating employees poorly is at some point they will check out mentally and emotionally and then you lose all hope of leveraging their strengths.

Here is yet another reason to treat employees well: as you grow into a strong Manager and Leader, there is a fair chance that you will be hiring and training your replacement as you move onward and upward. Would you want your team to be run by someone who treats them poorly and does not get their maximum performance?

As you proceed through your management career, there is also a chance that you will be hiring your replacement and someone you might ultimately report to. At that juncture, how will you want your future boss to respond to you as his employee?

CHAPTER 4

Are you more comfortable communicating with your team or would you rather be incommunicado?

If you lived alone on your own personal island, you could do whatever you wanted, as long as you were able to insure daily survival. On the other hand, imagine you were an air traffic controller, you would need to keep an open line of communication with the planes in the air, your co-workers, other flight towers, ground support staff, management, FAA, etc. Leadership is more akin to the flight control tower than living on a lonely island. If you want to make all the decisions, then start your own company and don't hire anyone. However, if you can't be a one-man-band, you need to create an environment where communication and open dialog is not only encouraged but required and rewarded.

A leader's ability to get tasks completed is directly related to the way the team perceives their leader's opinion of their worth and contributions. In other words, if the team thinks the leader sees them as a strong company asset, they will act accordingly. Conversely, if the team thinks the leader sees them as inferior, they will not perform to optimal levels. I (TD) recently worked for a company that overtly communicated their disdain for the sales team. The Division President could never figure out why they never attended the companies holiday events and more importantly why the company NEVER hit its sales goal – imagine? I have observed that people will rise or fall based on their leader's expectation of them, so keep the bar set high.

The next four categories deal with a leader's ability to get things done by their team. This starts with the leader's attitude. The right attitude toward your team will make it easy and fun to get tasks executed. The wrong attitude will do the opposite: you will make it difficult to get the team to buy into your vision or their objectives. Additionally, they certainly will not enjoy working for you.

13. Is 90% ok or do you feel no one but you can contribute 100%?

This was a challenge for me (TD) when I first got into management. I am a very detailed worker, planner, and goal setter. The program I developed for myself allowed me to be a high-income earner. When I became a department head, I had a hard time understanding why my reports didn't follow my example. I used to get frustrated until over time I realized a few things: 1-what worked so well for me may not work so well for everyone, 2-if they followed 90% of the program, they still came up winners and 3-I was less stressed by accepting 90% as long as it produced the needed results. Part of understanding this is realizing that high producers generally like to have some independence and input in their success. I learned this is a good thing as it indicates a healthy ego and a higher level of self-motivation. These are exactly the types of employees I want reporting to me. So the moral here is that if your direct report is not doing something exactly the way you would, it's often a positive not a negative. As long as the necessary results accrue, and as long as company policies are not contravened, be happy with the 90% and congratulate the team on their accomplishment.

14. Are you able to get tasks accomplished simply by asking or do you need to use manipulation and/or coercion?

I worked for a boss that felt he had to scare his managers into executing tasks. He came up with the most amazing stories — and occasionally threats - when all he had to do was just be open, honest and transparent. It's important to explain the benefits of a task from the company's perspective but it also goes a long way in getting buy-in when you share your thoughts, concerns, and motivations as well.

This is something that takes time to establish. It takes trust from you and for you and a track record of positive results. Once this level of leadership is established getting things done is a much less stressful.

15. Do you encourage open dialog or is it "my way or highway"?

I (TD) have found that in most situations open dialog is both appropriate and fruitful. Open dialog facilitates the completion of tasks and often creates a better outcome. This relates to many of the categories already mentioned, hiring the best, creating an open atmosphere and giving credit are a few tactics that will lead to open dialog.

Occasionally, you may not be able to allow additional input or discussion. A particular company edict or policy may not give you any room for your own interpretation or execution. In those cases, it is important to let the team know why there is no room for dialog. Tell them you hope they trust you enough to get the job done. Trust is so important in creating effective, harmonious working environments. If you have earned the trust of your team, you should be able to manage around these occasions where open dialog is not possible.

Autocratic leaders who operate on the "my way or the highway" theory of management will quite often get tasks completed. However, they will often get the minimum result from their team because their employees usually resent them and will avoid going the extra mile for their manager. The employee's behavior is chiefly motivated from fear and therefore they will only invest what is needed on any project and no more. Sadly, under this type of rule the company never prospers. Fear based motivation will not be productive over the long run.

16. Do you promote a team environment, or do you encourage conflict among your team?

Does this seem like a crazy question? It seems obvious that a manager who creates strife among his employees is destined to failure. Yet there are managers who feel it is necessary to pit one employee against another. This might be because the manager tries to keep everyone on guard and off balance.

This kind of management style is akin to the TV show "Survivor", with constantly shifting alliances and gamesmanship. It amazes me (EZ) when such a managerial style actually works in the short run. It is even more amazing when upper management is unaware of, or worse, actually condones this management style.

Legitimate competition among the team (for promotions, incentives, etc.) is not inherently bad, but when it is raised to the level of "survivor", it completely contradicts the Team concept. The movie "Glengarry Glen Ross" is a perfect example of Managerial Darwinism, as well as the negative behavior it fosters.

This management style is often the mark of an insecure, egotistic, or incompetent manager. If you are this type of manager, you will have little chance of moving into the Zone of Leadership. If you work for this type of manager, you need to find a new employer.

This conflict-fostering management style likely assumes you have a team of managers who are predisposed to lying and cheating. One particular boss used to ask me (TD) all the time if I was lying. The crazy thing was we used to catch him lying all the time. This illustrates an extreme example of hiring a team to surround us with people like us as opposed to hiring a team with diverse personalities and talents. This is an example of a manager who hired employees who were malleable and could be ruled by strife or who were open to creating conflict. I can tell you that under this kind of supervision you will have a very dysfunctional team. Everyone on the team will be looking over their shoulders to be wary of threats and booby-traps.

(EZ) There are many warning signs for a manager who likes to rule by strife:

The organizational chart is murky and/or fluid. I was once hired to run a department in a large corporation. The department had several directors and several managers working for each of those directors. A few months after I had the team organized to my satisfaction, I observed that one of my directors was falling behind on some of his tasks. The reason, he eventually explained, was that another VP (who was also my immediate supervisor and predecessor) had directed him to start work on a couple of projects without my knowledge. The other VP had previously managed this director, so he felt very comfortable in giving some work to my employee.

When I discussed this irregularity with my supervisor, he explained that he wanted the organizational chart to be fluid and based on his changing needs. I countered that I was hired to meet specific objectives, budgets, and goals, and that diverting my team from those would have a negative impact on the department's productivity and my team's incentives, not to mention my own.

Two things happened because of this conversation: 1. I was assured that my team incentives would not be harmed, and 2. My employee quickly learned how to justify his lack of productivity due to having two bosses. As you can imagine, this conflict did not have a happy or profitable ending!

Information for upper management is monitored, measured, and manipulated.

In another position, one of my tasks was to complete a monthly recap and a projection for the next month. This monthly report was rolled up into a final report by my supervisor, and then presented to upper management so they could keep track of production and get a quick forecast of the future. My supervisor made it a practice to not share his final report with his team. I was not concerned with this practice since I routinely hit my monthly projections and my report was never challenged. One day a senior VP happened to ask me how a particular project was proceeding. During our conversation, it became apparent that my report had been seriously manipulated by my supervisor. I discovered later that he referred to this practice as 'hiding the football', with the intent to keep senior management in the dark.

Directions and conversations are secretive.

With one particular supervisor, any conversation that began with "come into my office and close the door" typically involved malicious gossip or instructions that would undermine the efforts of another employee. The rest of the team quickly learned that a closed door was often the portent of managerial mischief.

Projects come and go without purpose, direction, or conclusion.

For whatever reason or intent, bad managers can set you up to fail. They may do this out of sheer ignorance or some Machiavellian plan. Whether the manager is incompetent or malicious, the net impact on your situation is the same, you fail. If you have a supervisor who directs you to research for weeks on a nebulous project, beware. If you have a manager who arbitrarily changes the parameters of a project midstream, beware. A good manager will give you good marching orders and will tell you what his expectations are for the project results and how they fit into the overall business plan.

Incentives and bonus plans are altered or suspended.

Some supervisors act as though the payment of an earned incentive is a budgetary failure. They act as though incentive monies due their employees will be coming out of their own pockets. There is incalculable damage to management credibility when incentive plans are arbitrarily and unilaterally modified or awarded in an unfair manner. When it becomes obvious that one employee has benefitted at the expense of another, the word spreads quickly among the troops.

I was on a sales team where incentives were totally mismanaged. Although the sales team would whoop and cheer as each sales promotion was unveiled, the cynics among us would yell "ABC" as the contest details were explained. Inevitably, the same 10% of the sales team would consistently win about two-thirds of the incentives. The contests were rigged for this kind of unfair pay-out because the manager who created the contest was clueless as to the impact of the metrics he had engineered. Obviously, the 10% were not going to reveal that the promotion was rigged in their favor. The 90% of the team that was shorted simply resigned themselves to an unfair program with the thought that a little bit of a bonus was better than none. And, perhaps, management would one day figure out how their statistics were skewed in favor of the 10%.

Management interpreted the cheers as positive reaction from the team, hungry for another incentive. In reality, the 90% were yelling "ABC" for a cynical reason. "ABC" stands for "Another Bogus Contest".

Performance reviews are breached.

As mentioned in the section titled "are you transparent or mysterious", I once had a supervisor who gave me a very good performance review, but then appended a note to his management that contradicted his positive evaluation of me. Postponed, retroactive, or post-dated performance reviews are a sign of an incompetent or malevolent manager. By the way, quarterly, mid-year and annual written performance reviews can be a great tool to communicate your expectations to individuals on your team and to discuss areas for performance improvement. By reviewing an individual's performance throughout the year, you give the employee the opportunity to course correct. I (TD) never understood why a manager would wait until the end of the year to let an employee know their performance was subpar or give them the opportunity through sage guidance ways to take them to an even higher performance level. A strong manager can wield the stick and the carrot in such a way that the individual can't wait to get back to work in a positive state of mind. This is another area where your HR Department can help you.

I (TD) have also had the pleasure of working for leaders who promoted a true team environment. I observed and enjoyed the benefits of a relaxed, but challenging, working environment. That group was one of the highest performing groups I have ever worked with. It was expected that behind closed doors we would challenge each other's ideas robustly and sometimes heatedly, but in the end, we walked out as a team. This kind of team cohesiveness doesn't happen overnight.

It takes time to hire the right mix of personalities and talents for your team. It is not unusual to change managers or to change their roles on your team. If you plan for the long-term success as you hire and train your team, you will find the finished product is well worth the effort.

17. Are you grateful for the results you get from your team, or do you believe it is expected?

Showing appreciation verbally, financially, or otherwise communicates to your staff that you value them and their contributions to the company. When I (TD) was very young and in one of my first jobs, my boss would hand each of us our weekly paychecks and tell us he really appreciated the work we performed the past week. I have never forgotten the feeling I experienced when he did that. It never got old because he was always sincere when he did it.

In today's world of direct deposit payroll it's hard to duplicate this effort. however, there are other ways to show your gratitude. One company I work with posts articles on social media every month showcasing their top producers.

Another time I experienced this kind of appreciation was when the owner of the company sent the managers a handwritten letter thanking us for tackling a very tough assignment. Ten years later I still have that letter!

Unfortunately, there are managers who just don't see the value to expressing gratitude. They believe the paycheck alone shows sufficient appreciation for a job well done. They are way off course on this belief; the paycheck is important, but it doesn't build relationships. In her book, Jesus as CEO, Laurie Beth Jones describes it this way, "Gratitude is a key element of leadership because gratitude means an open heart, a listening heart, a faith-filled heart."

Other ways of showing appreciation are bonuses, real time off, a donation made on behalf of the employee to the employee's charity of choice, etc. The benefits are so numerous to doing this it amazes me that some leaders still don't do it. Thanking employees for noteworthy results and milestones (completion of a challenging project, special customer service, setting a new sales record, birthdays, anniversaries, etc.) is more powerful when it is done in public. A written note as follow-up is also powerful.

The key to this technique is sincerity; your team will see right through you if you are just going through the motions. If you are not currently doing this or not doing much of it, I would challenge you to try start today. The results may surprise you.

Performance reviews can also be a good way to express gratitude and reinforce the behaviors you need for success. A good performance review will cover both positive and negative issues; it will also address needed areas of improvement. The areas needing improvement should include a plan for expected improvements with a timeline, specific targets, metrics, and upcoming dates for review points. Even a negative performance review should end with an expression of gratitude for anticipated positive change in performance.

While you are hiring and training your team, here is a formula for performance review (maybe on-boarding) (and expression of gratitude) that has served me (EZ) well:

End of first day: brief meeting with new hire to see how the first day went, any questions, thanks for taking the time for orientation, etc.

End of first week: ditto the above, expressing how glad you are that she is on the team, looking forward to solid future together, etc.

End of second week: ditto the above, noting early productivity achievements (including any suggestions to enhance performance), positive feedback from team-mates, immediate supervisor, etc.

End of first month: ditto the above, mention formal review point at 90 days and the type of metrics for that review,

End of second month: ditto the above

End of third month: formal probationary review, congratulations on achieving all metrics, absolutely delighted you are on the team, looking forward to continued results and success

End of sixth month: formal review for performance... maintain positive, constructive feedback and sincere gratitude for contributions to the team; mention the next formal review point at one year for performance and pay increase (including review of bonus/incentive plan)

All of these reviews should be short, to the point, and end on a positive note of thanks for solid performance and future expectations. The first five reviews should not have any elaborate paperwork or forms, but a short thank-you note to the employee with a brief recap of the discussion should be appreciated by the employee.

Your HR Department will likely have a written format for the 90 day, six month, and annual performance reviews. You should append a short thank-you note to the copy you provide to your employee post-interview.

This formula helped me build successful teams. It requires extra effort, and your gratitude must be sincere, but you will be rewarded with long term benefits for you and your team.

Another way to show gratitude is by mailing a gift card home to the employee's spouse or partner. This gift card can be used for a dinner or other treat. It should have a brief thank-you note to the spouse/partner saying how much you enjoy working with the employee and noting the special success that warranted the 'thank-you'. The contribution of spouses and partners are often overlooked, so this unexpected surprise will doubly reinforce your gratitude.

CHAPTER 5

Walking the Straight and Narrow

(TD) Walking the straight and narrow path is not always the easiest way to go. We always have options and how we choose those options determines our character. Character is often what we do when no one is watching. We can do the right thing or not, tell the truth or lie, put someone else's needs in front of ours or put our needs at the top. Often when money is involved doing the right thing becomes even more challenging. So how do we stay true to doing what it fair and just? We need something to keep us on course and hold us from drifting off or over the line; we need a moral compass and anchor. For me and my family it is our Christian faith. I believe that most religions, with the exception of some radical beliefs that promote hatred and violence, have a set of do's and don'ts, something akin to the Ten Commandments. These rules act as the sidelines or boundaries of a playing field; in other words, you can do what you want within those boundaries, but you can't cross over the side lines. As simple as it sounds, I have found that Leaders with a strong spiritual walk typically endeavor to do what is fair and just and that they make the strongest leaders. And they are usually more successful, and their departments are the most profitable and efficient.

When faced with decisions they run their options through their spiritual filters first, once they eliminate the bad choices, they are free to choose the best course of action from what is left knowing that it may not be the perfect answer, but it will stand up to the test of doing what is fair and just. This doesn't happen overnight, for me it came years after I made a commitment to read my bible every morning. Now it feels like it is on auto pilot, I'm not saying all my thoughts are pure or my actions are the best choice but when I am considering an option that is not fair and just, I simply don't get any rest. It just eats me up and I know pretty quickly that I need to revisit the issue.

Additionally, it helps to have an accountability partner; this can be your spouse, close friend, or a family member. The key is to have a partner that is open to letting you know when you start going sideways and brave enough to have tough conversations with you. For me it's my wife, my brother, and my best friend. I don't run every situation with all of them, but I always try to run it by at least two of them. Remember as I stated earlier there are very few decisions that must be made on the spot so give yourself time to vet through your options. Also remember the acrostic, "HALT(S)" (Hungry, Angry, Lonely, Tired, Sick); make sure you are in a good emotional and physical state when dealing with difficult situations.

I have observed and been a part of many decisions and I have found that it is actually easier to simply do the right thing. You will sleep better and most of all you will set an example that your team will want to emulate. In his book, *The*

21 Indispensable Qualities of a Leader, Maxwell says it this way, "Adversity is a crossroads that makes a person choose one of two paths: character or compromise. Every time he chooses character, he becomes stronger, even if that choice brings negative consequences."

CHAPTER 6

Get Them Fired Up

There is nothing that can fire up a team quicker than a leader with a high level of enthusiasm, passion and an unwavering belief in their abilities and the product or service you are selling. Earlier I stated that I believe there is a diminishing effect from the Leader down (remember the bonfire example). None is more apparent than leaders who have a "fire in their belly" for success. There will always be situations that are difficult, challenging or didn't work out the way you hoped, but a leader must be able to hold his head high, shake it off, learn from it and move on. Remember ALL eyes look up to you.

One sure fire way to ignite your team is to have productive meetings that always end on a high note. If you have to go over housekeeping issues that are not highly motivating, do it at the beginning of the meeting. Reserve the inspiring discussion for the end. That way you always finish on a high note.

I had a boss once who held the most bizarre sales meetings. He wound himself up to the point where, by the end of the meeting, he was yelling at the top of his lungs. He would end the meeting with the charge: "Now good luck and go out there and make some sales." After my first exposure to this harangue, I asked one of the tenured sales agents 'what just happened'? I will always remember his response: "Don't pay too much attention to him, he is always like that." The lesson here is that if you scream and yell all the time your team will become indifferent to you and your leadership.

Another technique that keeps a team energized is when other department managers mention to them that they appreciate the good job they are doing. I call this "cross pollinating". As a leader, hold your managers accountable for reaching out to team members in other departments. Additionally, as a leader have your boss reach out to your team from time to time with an uplifting compliment

Sadly, most supervisors and managers don't have a clue as to what motivates their teams. Much has been written about what motivates human beings. On a very basic level, Maslow's Hierarchy of Needs is good starting point. However, with the decades that have passed since his writing, and with the alphabet soup of Generations X, Y, Z and all their permutations, perhaps it is time for you to do some fresh research on what motivates your team.

As you speak to your employees, it never hurts to simply ask them 'what gets you really focused on doing your job, and then doing it even better?' You might be surprised with the answers.

To my (EZ) experience, base pay is a strong motivator, and a good incentive system is even better. If you have hired the right employee, she will work for the "cake" and give you excellent productivity. However, if you figure out the right "icing" for her, there will be no end to her 'above & beyond' efforts.

As a rule of thumb, know what your competitor's total employee compensation package is, and then beat it by 10%. As a result, you will always have a file of resumes from the top producers who will want to join your team as soon as you have an opening.

When you analyze your competitor's total package, be sure to include benefits and intangibles. I (EZ) once worked for a company that was paying well below competitive base salaries and we lost good candidates as a result. However, once our benefits and incentives were factored in, the net benefit to the candidate was significantly higher than that of our competition. We prepared a one-page graphic to illustrate our competitive advantage and we stopped losing candidates. We also shared it with current employees, and for many it became a Eureka moment.

Remember, incentives can cover a wide array of perks for your team: money, vacations, dinners, gift cards, perks for the spouse/partner, spas, a round of golf with the boss, and real time off. Real time off is often a huge benefit to the employee, yet most supervisors haven't a clue as to what it means.

Real time off means that there will not be stacks of work waiting for the employee's return. The thought of those stacks of work will be a real de-motivator and will put the employee in a mental hole while he contemplates the extra effort required upon his return.

Real time off also means that your employee will not have the need to be constantly checking voicemail, email, etc.

In a commission setting, real time off means that any leads that generate commission are preserved for the person who has earned the time off. As a Leader, imagine the impact you will have when you tell your team that they will have their leads and commissions protected while they enjoy the real time off, they have earned.

Never stop learning, training, and coaching. I (TD) have learned that we all have the capacity and desire to grow, and we will seek out organizations and leaders that will create that type of environment. In the book *Execution* by Larry Bossidy & Ram Charan they explain it this way, "Coaching is the single most important part of expanding others' capabilities. Good leaders regard every encounter as an opportunity to coach."

CHAPTER 7

Conclusion

Being a successful leader is both hard and easy. I have observed in myself and others that the hardest part is keeping the bar always raised no matter what the situation. As a former boss puts it, "Always take the high road." Once I made the commitment to simply do the right things, leadership became easy.

One of the biggest payoffs for me is when I see a direct report blossom into a great success. I take the responsibility of helping others reach their highest potential very seriously. Once the team sees your commitment to them, they will follow you because they know you not only have the company's best interests at heart, but theirs as well. Earlier Ed and I used the term, The Zone of Leadership, this is what we were referring to. Once you reach the Zone, there is no limit to the company's success. You will find yourself overwhelmed with resumes of people that want to be a part of your team. Everyone wants to be on a winning team, especially if that team has a good leader.

We hope this book helps you become an amazing leader. The world needs you now more than ever. And remember to pass it on. Help create leaders, help people grow and never stop learning and trying new techniques.

FINAL NOTES

Names and situations have been masked to protect the clue-less and even the Bozos. Some of the situations have been combined from several anecdotes.

He/she are interchangeable.

The Leaders and good Managers we have worked with will see themselves in these pages with positive affection... thanks to you all for being such good teachers—you know who you are! On the other hand, the Bozos are so clueless they will likely never touch this book.

APPENDIX 1 -
THE LEADER'S CHECK LIST

1- Would you say your manager leads by example:

Not very often	Most of the time	All the time
1	5	10

2- Would you say your manager is truthful and honest:

Not very often	Most of the time	All the time
1	5	10

3- Would say your manager keeps you in the loop:

Not very often	Most of the time	All the time
1	5	10

4- Do you have a clear understanding of what is expected from you:

Not very	Most of the time	All the time
1	5	10

5- Would say your manager is threatened by you:

Never	Some of the time	All the time
1	5	10

6- Would say your manager gives you the tools to reach your highest potential:

Not very often	Most of the time	All the time
1	5	10

7- Does your manger focus on your failures or your accomplishments:

Failures	Neither	Accomplishments
1	5	10

8- Does your manger give you credit for your ideas or take credit for your ideas:

Takes Credit	Neither	Gives Credit
1	5	10

9- Does your manager publicly praise your failures or your accomplishments:

Failures	Neither	Accomplishments
1	5	10

10- Does your manager encourage you to try new and innovate ways to improve your performance:

Not very often	Most of the time	All the time
1	5	10

11- Would say your manager is your cheer leader or your buzz killer:

Buzz Killer	Neither	Cheerleader
1	5	10

12- Does your manager encourage you to continually improve so you can achieve your highest level of performance:

Not very often	Most of the time	All the time
1	5	10

13- Do you feel your manager requires you to complete tasks exactly the way he would tackle them:

All the time	Some of the time	Most the time
1	5	10

14- Do you think your manager feels like the only way to complete assigned tasks is to threaten, manipulate or coerce you:

All of the time	Some of the time	Never
1	5	10

15- Would you say your manager encourages you to share your ideas and then **incorporate** them into the business plan:

Not very often	Most of the time	All the time
1	5	10

16- Would you say your manager encourages a Team environment:

Not very often	Most of the time	All the time
1	5	10

17- Does your manger show gratitude for your accomplishments:

Not very often	Most of the time	All the time
1	5	10

BIBLIOGRAPHY

Zig Ziglar, *Over the Top* (Nashville: Thomas Nelson, Inc Publishers, 1994)

John C Maxwell, *The 21 Irrefutable Laws of Leadership* (Tennessee: Thomas Nelson, Inc., 2002)

Jack Welch, *Winning* (New York: HarperCollins Publishers Inc., 2005)

Jim Collins, *Good to Great* (New York: HarperCollins Publishers Inc., 2001)

Tom Peters, *In Search of Excellence* (New York: HarperCollins Publishers Inc 1982)

Zig Ziglar, *See you at the Top* (Louisiana: The Pelican Publishing Company, Inc., 1975)

Laurie Beth Jones, *Jesus as CEO*, (New York: Hyperion, 1995)

John C Maxwell, *The 21 Indispensable Qualities of a Leader* (Tennessee: Thomas Nelson, Inc., 1999)

Larry Bossidy & Ram Charan, *Execution* (New York: Crown Business, 2002)